Midnight Sun Oracle

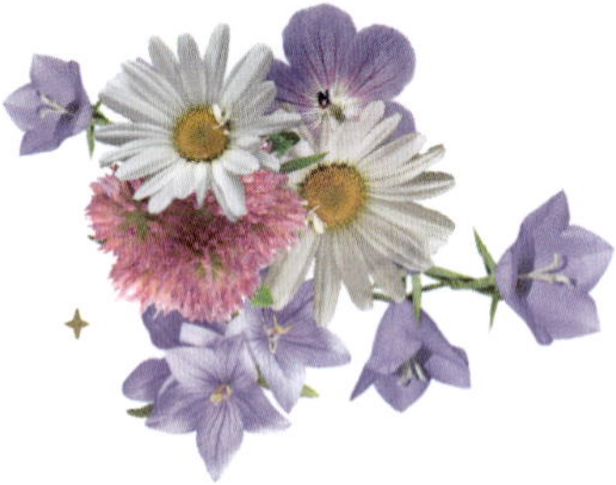

Midnight Sun Oracle

SELENA MOON

Magical Messages *from* the Nordic Midsummer

ROCKPOOL

A Rockpool book
PO Box 252
Summer Hill
NSW 2130
Australia

rockpoolpublishing.com
Follow us! **f** 🅾 rockpoolpublishing
Tag your images with #rockpoolpublishing

ISBN: 9781922786036

Published in 2024 by Rockpool Publishing
Copyright text and images © Selena Moon 2024
Copyright design © Rockpool Publishing 2024

All rights reserved. No part of this publication may be reproduced,
stored in a retrieval system, or transmitted in any form or by
any means, electronic, mechanical, photocopying, recording or
otherwise, without the prior written permission of the publisher.

Design and typesetting by Alissa Dinallo, Rockpool Publishing
Edited by Brooke Halliwell

Printed and bound in China
10 9 8 7 6 5 4 3 2 1

Contents

INTRODUCTION		03
HOW TO USE THE CARDS		05
SPREADS		06
THE CARDS		13
1.	Maypole	14
2.	Wreath	16
3.	Red clover	18
4.	Bluebell	20
5.	Marguerite	22
6.	Ring dance	24
7.	Singing	26
8.	Feast	28
9.	Belonging	30
10.	Bright night	32
11.	Country road	34
12.	Midnight swim	36
13.	Summer romance	38
14.	Frogs	40
15.	Children	42

16.	Rain	44
17.	Lover's dream	46
18.	Pentathlon	48
19.	June	50
20.	Skinny dipping	52
21.	Holiday	54
22.	Strawberries	56
23.	Oak	58
24.	Magical night	60
25.	Midsummer broom	62
26.	Bare feet	64
27.	Celebration	66
28.	Sunset	68
29.	Heat	70
30.	Juicing	72
31.	Healing power	74
32.	Midsummer night's treasure	76
33.	Future divination	78
34.	Dress	80
35.	Spirits and drinks	82
36.	Midnight sun	84

ABOUT THE CREATOR 87

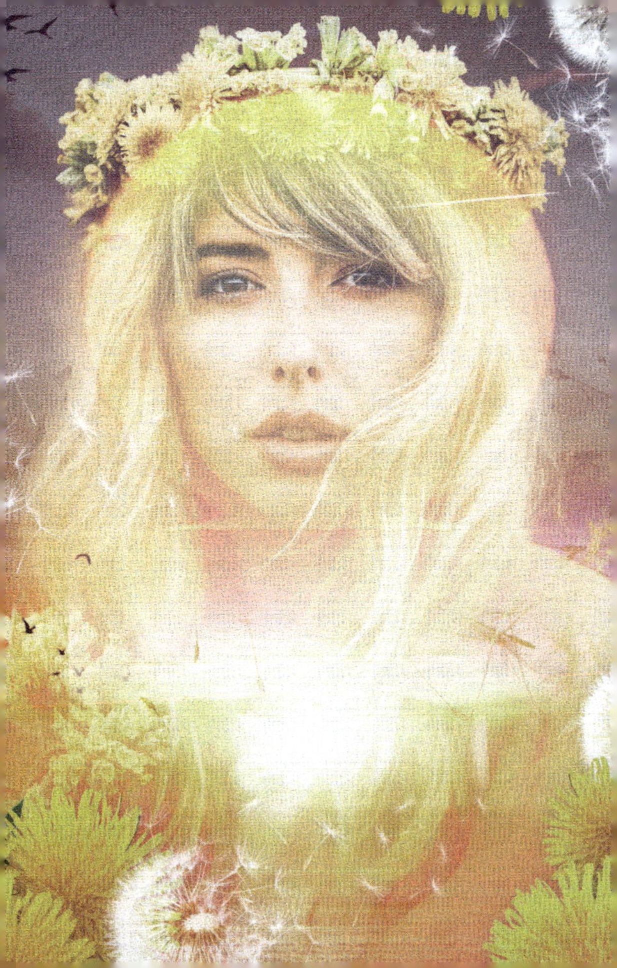

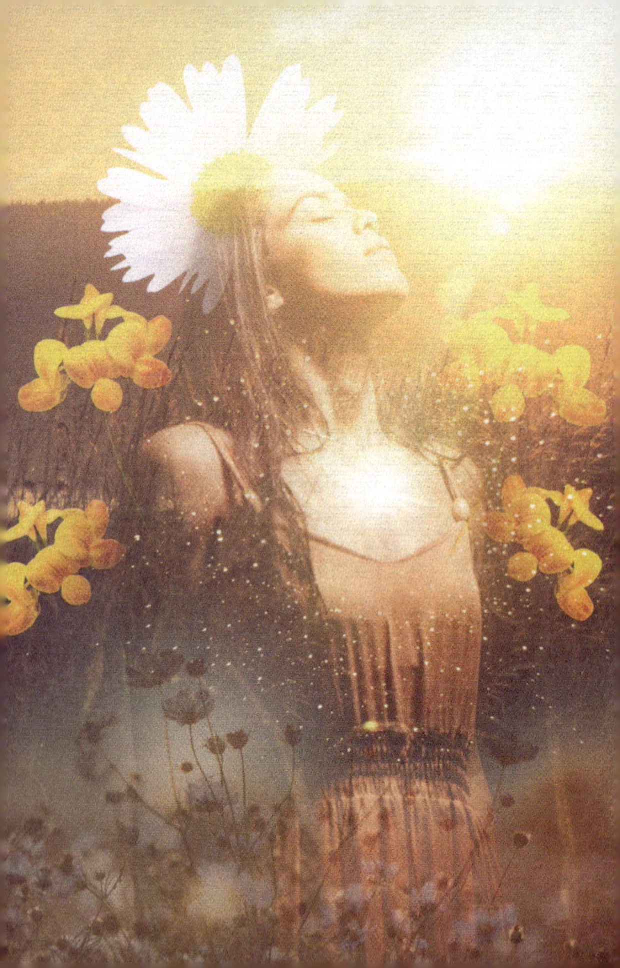

Introduction

Welcome to the Midsummer magic! This deck is derived from the themes of Midsummer celebrations hailing from the Nordic European countries. It is also known as Litha in the pagan wheel of the year.

Midsummer is a family tradition and a celebration of summer, light and love. Traditionally Midsummer is celebrated around the summer solstice where the day is the longest and the night the shortest. From the north pole down to about 60 degrees latitude, the sun never fully sets and day and night join as one, hence the beautiful midnight sun can be experienced.

In Sweden and Finland, Midsummer is a public holiday and since 1953 Midsummer's Day always occurs on the Saturday between 20 and 26 June and Midsummer's Eve on the Friday before. However, some other European countries still celebrate Midsummer on John the Baptist's birthday on 24 June.

It has not been established whether Midsummer was celebrated BC but the church started celebrating the birth of John the Baptist around 300AC. It is written in the Bible that John the Baptist was born six months after

Christ and is therefore celebrated on 24 June, which is the date Midsummer used to be celebrated.

Growing up in Sweden, the Midsummer celebration was one of the biggest highlights of the year and always involved a lot of fun, food, family and friends and magical moments. Even though the tradition changes over the years between families and regions, the overall messages still stand and I hope to bring these messages to you through this deck.

As a child, I never acknowledged what we were celebrating and why, I was just happy to have a holiday and enjoyed spending time with my family and friends. I find this common even in adult life where we often neglect the meaning of things and I think we have a lot to gain by remembering what we celebrate.

The purpose of this deck is to bring back the messages and meanings of the traditions, symbols, rituals and activities that we associate with Midsummer and to give you energy and inspiration through the love and light that Midsummer brings.

This deck is deeply inspired by my own experiences of Midsummer and I wish to share with you the enchanting power of this beautiful season.

How to use the cards

This deck is designed to bring the energy of Midsummer to you. Regardless of the time of year or if you celebrate this season you can benefit from using these cards. Use this deck whenever you feel drawn to it or if you need guidance, clarity or inspiration. You can use it in whatever fashion you prefer. You could pull random cards to see what message the deck has for you, ask the deck specific questions or you can use any card spreads that are not solemnly designed for tarot decks only. You can also use the spreads suggested in this booklet or come up with your own.

Each card has two main keywords but I encourage you to find your own meaning by studying the imagery and seeing what resonates with you, what you see in the cards and what meaning you can take from it.

All the visuals for each card are created to inspire intuitive reading with multiple symbols incorporated for you to draw inspiration from. If you feel the need or want a deeper understanding of each card you can read about the meaning of each card in this booklet.

Spreads

As mentioned earlier you can use this deck for any type of spread both complicated and simple. If you are new to reading you may want to start with familiarising yourself with the deck by pulling cards randomly or pulling one card at a time based on a question.

You could also use some simple spreads such as a two-card spread to get a broader answer to a question or a three-card spread that represents past, present and future or a problem, the root cause and a possible solution.

Below you will find four different card spreads specifically created based on the Midsummer tradition but you can use them at any time.

WREATH SPREAD

This is a spread for self-love. Use this spread whenever you are feeling down and need to love yourself a bit more or whenever you feel a need to fill your own cup.

    Card 1: something I love about myself.
    Card 2: what my best friends see in me.
    Card 3: what my family appreciates me for.
    Card 4: I am good at this.
    Card 5: this is my strongest trait.

SEVEN FLOWERS SPREAD

Find out more about your existing or future lover with this spread.

Card 1: what is this person like as a friend?
Card 2: what is this person like as a partner?
Card 3: what is this person like as a lover?
Card 4: what is the overall energy of this person?
Card 5: how will I connect with this person?
Card 6: what does this person offer me?
Card 7: what can I offer this person?

MAYPOLE SPREAD

Use this spread to help you acknowledge something you need to focus on more and to get insight on how to do so.

Card 1: the root of my current situation.
Card 2. what I need to focus on.
Card 3: what I can use to help me focus.
Card 4: a possible outcome of refocusing.
Card 5: my biggest asset that can help me to refocus.

MIDNIGHT SUN SPREAD

Use this spread to find appreciation and inspiration for your life.

Cards 1, 2 and 3: what are some of the most beautiful things in my life?
Card 4: what do I want to create more of in my life?
Card 5: how can I create more of the things discovered in card 4?
Card 6: what are some possible things to gain from creating more of these?

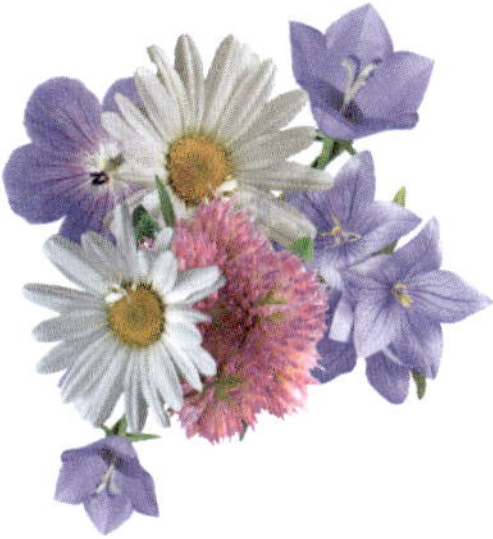

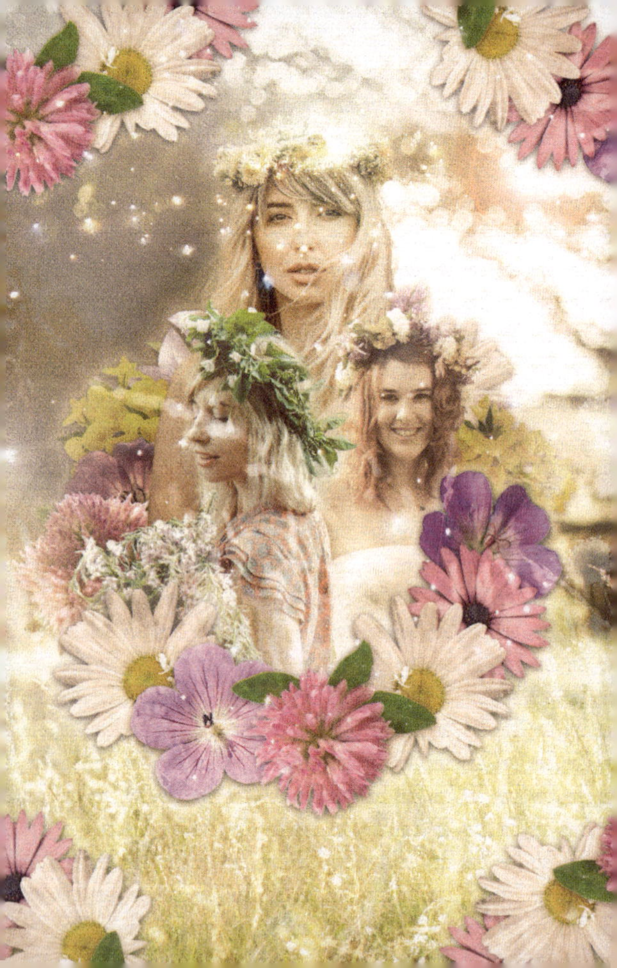

The Cards

1 ✦ Maypole

MANIFESTATION · PRIDE

Dressed in beautiful greenery and flowers to manifest fruitfulness and growth the maypole is a proud figure in the middle of the meadow. A strong symbol for this special celebration, it is raised by the people of the land as a preparation for the celebration that is about to take place and as a host of the day.

The maypole becomes the centre of attention for all the guests who come to celebrate together as they build and raise this point of gravity to dance and play around it. It is the most important attribute and symbol of Midsummer. The maypole is made of wood, dressed in leaves and comes in different shapes, but the most usual is a vertical pole with a horizontal beam to form a cross and a wreath of flowers or leaves hanging from each end of the beam.

MESSAGE

Like the maypole, it's time for you to be in focus. Have you neglected yourself recently? It may be beneficial for you to re-evaluate some things in your life and make sure that you prioritise yourself. Let you be the centre of attention for once. And just like the maypole we all come in different shapes, sizes and appearances, but nonetheless we are all beautiful. Know and celebrate your unique appearance. Let yourself be seen as you are, accept the love and attention you get from others and be proud of who you are.

The maypole is not just a pretty decoration; it is also considered a token of good growth and a rich harvest for the year ahead. Therefore, this may also be a sign that prosperity is on the way for you; your hard work has paid off and wealth is on the way.

2 • Wreath

SELF-LOVE · BEAUTY

The women are roaming the land in search of the most beautiful wildflowers to create a wreath to be worn by mothers, daughters and children on this special day. Blues, reds, whites and yellows are intertwined in a magical ritual of binding with each woman using their own technique. Friends and family join in, dancing and running around while the women of Midsummer craft the headpieces.

Women proudly wear the flower crown, embracing the royal feeling throughout the day and making every woman feel special, unique and celebrated. This day, all women get to be the queen of Midsummer.

MESSAGE

Let the energy of the wreath bring you the sensation of self-love and embrace the beauty of your life. Take a moment to list the things you love about yourself. What makes you feel beautiful and healthy? Can you do more of those things?

Nature is believed to possess the most power during Midsummer when everything is in full bloom and growth is at its peak. We capture this special force in the flower wreath in the hope of maintaining health and keeping illnesses and misery away. Channel the power of nature through the wreath and let it bring you good health and joy.

3 + Red clover

ABUNDANCE · CULTIVATION

Red clover grows in abundance alongside the country roads, in the meadows and around the edges of the forest. It spreads like a beautiful pink blanket that warms your soul. In bouquets it harmonises, in meadows it thrives, on plates it fills and in wreaths it shines.

As clover blooms between June and August in the northern hemisphere, it peaks around the time of

Midsummer. It is one of the most common pea plants to be cultivated by farmers. Usually harvested before it blooms, it is used as feed for horses, cows and other farm animals.

MESSAGE

The strong colour of red clover brightens the fields as well as your heart, so embrace its positive energy to feel more energised in your life. Imagine the intense colour of deep pink filling your body, letting it run through you and feeling its power igniting you with life.

The flowers and leaves are edible for people as well as animals and can be used in salads or made into flour. Red clover never stops giving, so take this as a reminder to share your qualities with others; show your love and give your energy to others as well as yourself.

9 + Bluebell

RARITY · APPRECIATION

Known in Sweden as big bluebell (*Campanula persicifolia*), these sweet wildflowers stand tall in the country road ditches – a rarity to stumble upon, a beautiful sight when finally found. If you persevere you may just get rewarded with the gift of the bluebell's appearance. Their welcoming shape invites you in, making you feel special and giving you a grin.

The bluebell thrives in warm temperatures and therefore makes its appearance during summer in the Nordic countries. Sweden's national flower, it is beloved for its stunning blue tints and soft shape; therefore, it makes an obvious appearance in Midsummer celebrations.

MESSAGE

Worn in your hair or intertwined in your wreath, the sacred beauty of the bluebell becomes one with you. Embrace its precious energy, let it fill you with pride and appreciation for yourself. You are worthy, you are beautiful and you are rare.

If you have been a bit harsh on yourself or others lately, take this card as an indication to soften your outlook. Be kind and gentle and you may find more appreciation instead of distress.

5 ✦ Marguerite
GIFT · ANSWERS

Often neglected and not seen, the marguerite is what brings out the beauty in all the other flowers around it. With its many long white petals, it acts as a separator between the other colours, making them stand out more.

Even though in some countries this flower is considered a weed, it would not be a Midsummer without it. It makes its appearances in flower wreaths, as pot plants and as gifts.

MESSAGE

This card is an indication that you may have neglected someone in your life, be it a friend, family member or yourself. It's time to acknowledge what you bring to people and what you can bring to yourself. Take the time to reflect on what you have contributed to other people's lives. If you have been harsh on yourself lately, try to see yourself as a gift to others.

On Midsummer, it is also common to use these flowers to predict if your love interest loves you back by picking the petals one by one and alternating saying 'loves me' and 'loves me not' for each petal you pull. The last one you pull out is your answer. If you have an active love interest, this card indicates that it may be time for you to find out if they love you back. Getting a definite answer can sometimes feel better than being oblivious, regardless of what their answer may be.

6 + Ring dance
ACTION · FUN

A joyous event on Midsummer is the traditional dancing around the maypole. Holding each other's hands and forming a circle around the maypole we all become one as we create the dance. There are typical songs and choreographed moves that are a tradition to perform during this day of celebrations. Families will have their own favourites and customs but the common theme is love, laughter and a time to be silly.

MESSAGE

You can create the energy of the ring dance in your life. If you have been feeling a bit dull or uninspired this is an indication for you to gather your loved ones and do some activities together. Perhaps even try something new that you haven't done before to get more inspiration in your life.

The ring dance is mainly a fun event for the children, but it is also an opportunity for the adults to be childish and let go of perfection and performance that often comes with work and home and life duties. See if you can channel your inner child, let loose and allow yourself to be carefree and happy, to let go of other people's expectations of you and try not to worry about what other people think.

7 + Singing
CONNECTION · OUTLET

Singing is part of the traditional ring dance as well as around the dinner table on Midsummer's Eve. Common themes we sing about are the beautiful season we are celebrating, animals, love and joy. It's a time for everyone to connect, join our voices together and create this magical feeling of belonging, family and love. No matter who you are, where you come from or your ability to sing, you can join in and be a part of creating connection through your voice.

MESSAGE

Like singing together, is there something you can do to encourage love and belonging in your life? Think about whether there is something you can do through your voice to create more or deeper connections with the people you care about.

Singing is also about joining together as one and leaving judgement and pressure behind. Whether it be singing or something else, you can use this as an inspiration to find a more relaxed attitude if you have been feeling anxious or if you often find yourself in a pressured situation.

Perhaps you need to find an outlet for something you feel pressured about. Like the notes coming out when singing, what can you use to let out what you've been holding inside?

8 + Feast
INDULGENCE · CONTRIBUTION

As with any other big holiday or seasonal celebration, there is no Midsummer without a lot of food and feasting with your family and friends. It is common to have a buffet with many food options or a bring-your-own setup where everyone contributes and shares what they brought. As it's summer, seafood is common to see on the dinner table – especially pickled herring, which is a signature dish on the Swedish Midsummer buffet.

MESSAGE

The feast is a means to connect and share joy and love and to enjoy the highlights of this season. Food serves as a reason to bring people together and the feast tells you to indulge and enjoy life to the fullest and to connect with your loved ones over a meal.

It shows you that you have an abundance of options to enjoy in your life and you don't necessarily need to follow what you have been taught – you can come up with your own ideas and options to enjoy your life to the fullest.

The feast has something for everyone: nobody needs to feel left out or unsatisfied. Sharing the food is sharing love, so take the opportunity to do the same and make sure you contribute to and enjoy the people in your life.

9 ✦ Belonging
TOGETHERNESS · WELCOMING

Midsummer is a time for everyone to enjoy, bringing all kinds of people together. Whether a family member, a neighbour, a friend or a visitor, all are welcome to share the experience, no matter their age, gender or where they're from. The tradition invites you to share the rituals, games and food with everyone to experience a sense of belonging.

Regardless of how the day is celebrated and what events are incorporated, the point is that it's done together, whether it be decorating the maypole, binding wreaths, cooking, playing games or dancing.

MESSAGE

This card may be an indication that you need to create more sense of belonging in your life or in someone else's, so take a look at the common activities in your life and evaluate if they can be a shared experience to access the energy that belonging can bring.

Have you noticed someone in your surroundings feeling a bit lost or being a bit of an outsider? This is a sign for you to welcome them in and share the love and community that you possess. Perhaps invite them along to the things you like to enjoy or offer your support if that's what they need.

Remember it's not always about what you do, just that you do something and you are doing it together.

10 + Bright night
ENCHANTING · DISCOVERY

Midsummer is a celebration of the summer solstice. The date when the day is the longest and the night the shortest. The further up north you go, the longer amount of daylight you will experience, and in some parts the sun barely goes down before it starts to rise again. To experience this is truly mesmerising.

As the opposite happens in the winter months, where it's almost constantly dark, this phenomenon brings out the energies of enchantment and positivity, allowing you to focus on the most magical aspects of your life right now and see them, acknowledge them and enjoy them even more.

MESSAGE

If you have experienced a period of darkness, know that brighter times will come and the dark cycle shall end. Hang in there and try and focus on the positive things you know for certain that you have or that are to come.

This card may also be an indication that something has been hidden from you for a while and is about to come to light. It may be a new perspective that helps you to stay positive or to see things more clearly and in detail and that will help you to know where to go next.

Know that there are positive times ahead regardless of what you may have just discovered.

11 + Country road
IMPERFECTION · JOURNEY

This festive season is often celebrated in the countryside. It's not uncommon for people living in the city to make their way to rural places to enjoy nature in a more peaceful location. Part of Midsummer is celebrating summer and all that comes with it, such as blossoms, bright nights, warmth, and time to relax and rewind. Driving along winding country roads as you slowly make your way to the awaiting oasis of country living, festivities and friends contributes to the beautiful feeling of peace, rest and reset.

MESSAGE

The journey is part of the goal and is there for you to enjoy, not to quickly pass and get over with to reach the end, so take your time to appreciate the effort you are making to achieve something.

The road is also there for you to feel and experience a very physical connection to nature: feeling and hearing the gravel under your feet, feeling the curves of nature, seeing and smelling wildflowers along the way. Just like life, the country road comes with bumps and imperfections, but that is also part of its beauty and experience. Therefore, be mindful of judging in your own life and make sure to appreciate the here and now as well as the road you had to walk to get here and the road you have ahead.

12 + Midnight swim
FREEDOM · SELF-SUFFICIENCY

There are few things that feel as magical as a midnight dip in the lake or the ocean. In northern countries, this is seldom an option as the weather is too cold but during the Midsummer holiday if you are lucky the seasons have been warm enough to enable you to bathe in the water.

There is something forbidden about going out in the water late at night which brings the exquisite feeling of power over yourself and your decisions. Making your way to the water's edge with nobody around to see or hear you, the dark yet calm water, dipping your toe first to feel the temperature to then succumb silently brings on the feeling of being totally free. Free of judgement, free of rules and free of other people's power over you. There is just you and the water and perhaps a special friend that you chose to share this experience with.

MESSAGE

If you have been feeling restricted in any area of your life, this card is an indication for you to break free and break some unwritten rules. Take a deep look inside yourself and ask what your heart and soul are craving right now.

Let yourself be you and work on being comfortable in your own skin. Regardless of the influences around you, you are the narrator of your life and you have the power to give yourself moments of freedom.

13 · Summer romance
LOVE · LUST

Love is in the air! The summer season brings out the emotions of love and lust, everyone is out and about and feeling positive and happy to finally shed their winter clothes and come out of their shells. It's the perfect time to meet someone special and share some sparkling moments together.

It's a time for parties and gatherings and meeting new people, which also increases the chances of finding love or a new special connection with someone.

MESSAGE

This card is an indication that there is potential for a new connection to form or an existing one to change or grow.

If you have the opportunity, it may be a good idea to accept invitations and give yourself a chance to meet new people or for you to open the door and invite people in, both in a practical and emotional way.

If you have already found love in your life and are in a relationship this is a good time for you to grow that connection further. See if you can find a way to bring the initial feelings you had with this person to the surface again. There's no greater feeling than the excitement and tingle of falling in love, but those feelings fade and grow into something else the longer you stay together. That doesn't mean it's impossible to access again. Try and remember what you did together in the beginning. Can you relive some moments or can you come up with new ideas to try together to bring in more passion and lust to the relationship again?

14 • Frogs
SELF-EXPRESSION · CAREFREE

Frogs often possess magical powers in fables and children's stories and likewise they are represented during Midsummer. It is common to see them around this season and one of the most common songs during the dance around the maypole is about frogs and the funny fact that they don't have either ears or tails.

MESSAGE

Embrace the energy of the frog and welcome your childish side, be free and express yourself no matter how silly it might be. It's a time for fun and games and to be free of judgement. Dance like nobody is watching, sing like nobody is listening and let your creative side out in the open.

Frogs also symbolise transformation or rebirth and we've all heard the story about the princess kissing the frog who will then transform into a prince. If you've pulled this card, it may be an indication that you need to make a change and enter a new state in your life. Perhaps you need to embrace your carefree side, focus on what you really want and ignore what other people might think. Throw any judgements about others and yourself out the door and transform into the better version of yourself.

15 ✦ Children
GIVING · PLAYFULNESS

Even though we all celebrate Midsummer no matter what age, the children really make the day extra special. They bring out love and warmth in the people around them and everyone makes an extra effort to give them a lovely time during this holiday season. Children bring their playful energy and spread it around and as much as they give to us, we want to give back to them.

During Midsummer's Eve, children also help to make the games more engaging, the meals more unpredictable and light-hearted and they truly bring a magical atmosphere to the celebrations.

MESSAGE

This card indicates that you may need to evaluate the balance between giving and taking in your life. Have you been lacking the energy to give and share your love with other people? If you find you have been giving too much and it's starting to drain you, you could benefit from finding new motivation and inspiration or perhaps just taking a break to get back on the right track again.

Children also represent innocence, pure joy and non-judgement, so this card can also indicate the need to bring out your inner child more. If you have been judging yourself or feeling judged by others, are stuck in a rut or having less fun in your life than you would like this is a nudge for you to access your playful side and take time to have some fun!

16 ✦ Rain

CLEANSING · EMOTIONS

Ironically, it often rains on Midsummer even though it's supposed to be in the middle of summer with lovely weather and sunshine. A standing joke in Swedish culture is talking about 'Midsummer weather', meaning miserable, rainy and colder than it's supposed to be!

MESSAGE

Rain doesn't have to be a negative thing and the celebrations still go ahead to the best of our abilities regardless of the weather. And you can do the same thing in life. Sometimes circumstances change that you are not in control of but still do the best that you can. Use the new circumstances to your benefit. How can you take advantage of the situation and create a desirable outcome?

Rain also symbolises emotions and flow. Water is cleansing, so this card indicates that a clean-out can be beneficial. Let your emotions flow, don't try to control them. If you need to cry, cry. If you need to scream, do so! Whatever emotions you might be feeling right now, let them come forward, sit with them, acknowledge them, thank them then let them pass through. Let this process cleanse you so you can feel refreshed and not bogged down by heavy feelings.

17 • Lover's dream
PRESENT MOMENT · DREAM

There is a mythical story about how to dream of your future loved one. The story tells you to collect seven flowers of different kinds as you jump over seven round pole fences. You then place these seven flowers under your pillow and when you go to sleep you will dream about your future love.

MESSAGE

We often get caught up in our lives and fantasise a lot about the person we are going to spend our life with, keep analysing the people we meet or even hope that it is the one person that we currently dream of. But with the mindset of the seven flowers lover's dream you can open your mind to the possibility that your future partner might be someone you haven't even met yet. Keep the mystery in your love life and be open to whatever happens.

It might seem as if this act tells you to focus on your future, but surrendering to the present moment may be what is going to give you the future you are dreaming of. Being open to the idea that you cannot know who will enter your life, at what point in time and what impact they will have on you, yet knowing at the same time it is okay to zone out, to dream of what you want and to manifest your own dream life as long as it doesn't cloud your current happiness.

18 · Pentathlon

TEAMWORK · EXPLORATION

A common element in the Midsummer celebrations is pentathlons or similar types of small games for all ages to enjoy. There might be teams and competitions created for the sake of having fun and getting to know and socialise with all the guests involved. If the celebration is big with a lot of guests this is the perfect ice breaker to get people to engage with one another, especially with the people they may not already know. It's a great way to mix different ages and learn from each other.

MESSAGE

The games are all about teamwork and playing to each other's strengths. Do you know what your strengths are? Think about what you contribute the most in your group of friends and likewise, what are the strengths of your friends and about how this is beneficial in your life.

You can also embrace the idea of exploring new ground with people in your life. Be open to learning and engaging with people you might not normally socialise with. It might be a good idea to search outside your usual group of friends; be curious and see what you find.

19 • June

BEGINNINGS · BALANCE

Midsummer's Eve, the designated day for the celebration of Midsummer, always falls on the third Friday of the month of June. In the northern hemisphere, June represents the start of summer, the start of holidays and the start of something a lot of people have been looking forward to. June is a month of beginnings, of relief, of hopes and dreams.

MESSAGE

This card symbolises the excitement and anticipation that new beginnings bring. This is all positive energy and you can benefit from channelling this energy at any point in your life. If you need a new start on something or need to feel excited again, this is an indication that you can create that for yourself and you don't need to wait for a specific time or moment for this to happen.

June, being the sixth month of the calendar year, also symbolises harmony and balance. This could be an indication that you should focus on creating or maintaining harmony in your life. If something is off balance see what you can do to bring it back to a stable state.

20 • Skinny dipping
NON-JUDGEMENT • SELF-CARE

A warm and bright summer evening is the perfect invitation for skinny dipping. It's still hot in the evening and not many people are out, the celebrations have finished and as it's often in a secluded area it lends itself perfectly to enjoy a private moment.

There is an immense feeling of freedom as the water surrounds your whole body. It's a moment for yourself to be the authentic you, just like you were born to be. You and your naked body, without anyone's judgement and most importantly without self-judgement.

MESSAGE

This card symbolises the true and naked self. Who you really are when you take the outer world out of the equation: the things you own, the people in your life, what you do for work or as a hobby, the struggles and pains. Embrace who you are as a person and see if you can find an oasis in your life where there's space for you to just be you. Where you are not being judged by anyone and where you can really feel yourself and appreciate who you are deep down inside.

This is a call for self-love and care, to hold and to nurture your inner child and to truly see yourself first, surrendering to your authentic self and enjoying being with yourself.

21 • Holiday
RELAXATION · POSITIVITY

Midsummer's Eve is a public holiday and it's very common for people to take the whole week off work to go and enjoy this holiday with their family and friends. Holidays symbolise relaxation, a break from your day-to-day life and a time to enjoy yourself doing things just the way you prefer without having to feel stressed by obligations and to-do lists.

MESSAGE

This card invites you to bring some holiday energy into your life. We spend a lot of time focusing on tasks and must-do's but see if you can also focus a bit on the things you love to do, the things you enjoy, the things that make time fly. If you were to get some time off right now, what would you do?

Is there anything you can do to give yourself small holidays in your normal week? Can you plan it differently so that you have bigger chunks of time to 'do nothing', meaning doing the things you would do when you are on a holiday?

This card may also be an indication that you have been going and going and haven't taken the time that you deserve to appreciate life. You may need to slow down, reflect and have a moment for yourself to inject some positivity and motivation back into your life.

22 ✦ Strawberries

ATTENTION · FERTILITY

Sweet, sun-kissed strawberries are a must on Midsummer, whether they serve as decoration on a cake, are enjoyed with ice cream or eaten just as they are. It is only in summertime when we can enjoy local Scandinavian strawberries that are not imported from more southern countries and it makes the occasion extra special.

MESSAGE

With their bright red colour, delicious flavour and scent, strawberries call for your attention. They show you the path to love, pleasure and fruition. Have you lost your way recently and need to step back and notice something you have missed? There may be someone trying to become close to you or trying to show you love; are you letting them?

Enjoying local produce can help you reconnect with the land and feel the appreciation of where you came from and for nature as a whole. There are so many things that are given to us by Earth, and this is a moment for you to see the small things and watch the enjoyment that it brings. Therefore, if you haven't recently, this is a call for you to look around you and look to your roots to find love and appreciation.

With many little seeds incorporated into their skin, strawberries are also a symbol of fertility. This card can indicate that it is a good time to plant a new seed and try and grow something new. If there is something you've always wanted to create in your life, it could be a good time to take the initial step.

23 + Oak

STABILITY · STRENGTH

Oak is a common species of tree in the northern hemisphere; robust and grand, its leaves are commonly used to dress up the maypole. With its massive trunk and tall, wide crown, the oak symbolises stability, something to lean on, strength and endurance. The oak is always welcoming and giving, it invites children to play by functioning as a playground, it gives its leaves for decoration and produces acorns.

MESSAGE

Just like the oak, we can also be the stability for someone. We can provide strength and be welcoming and giving to everyone around us. Do you have any oaks in your life and are you being someone else's oak? Think about what you can do to manifest the power of the oak in your life and in other people's lives. Maybe by always being there to listen to someone or providing a safe space or just being someone to have fun with and helping them to forget about wherever problems might be present in their life.

Know that you can always access the security of the oak and channel its energy. If you don't have any oaks around, you can visualise them in your mind or go out in nature and seek that feeling from other trees; they are all connected through the earth.

24 • Magical night
LIMITLESS • PEACE

Something truly special about this time of year in Scandinavia is the long, bright nights. There is something very magical about an evening that goes on forever and just keeps giving. You have the same sense of relaxation and enjoyment you would feel on a regular evening but it lasts double the time as the sun sets extremely late.

MESSAGE

This is the moment to be with yourself and enjoy the time you have, regardless of what you are doing. You can create a magical night for yourself whenever you want. Tap into the mindset of unlimited options or opportunities. What is it that makes you feel your most relaxed or what do you do to enjoy your evenings? Perhaps it's time for you to reset and start enjoying the free time you have when you are done with work, housework, studies or whatever obligations you have in life and make the most out of the spare time that you have.

You have the power to create a space and moment that is only for you. If there is turbulence in your life, you have the ability to create your own peace, even if it's just for a moment. If you've rushed through life lately and not taken the time to stop and focus on your 'me-time', this is an indication for you to do so.

25 ✦ Midsummer broom

CLEARING · PROTECTION

Preparations are a big part of Midsummer celebrations and part of that is making sure your house is clean. Traditionally brooms made out of different materials from nature were used to sweep the floors of the homes to get them Midsummer ready.

The broom could consist of branches of birch and different kinds of dried flowers or leaves. Back in the day, it was a common belief that the Midsummer broom had magical powers and possessed the ability of protection.

MESSAGE

This card may be an indication that you have some negative energy in your life or in your home that needs to be cleared out. Sometimes we procrastinate for too long and get overwhelmed by the things we need to do. Cleaning up and clearing out is a good way to bring back motivation and get the feeling of a clean slate and you could find yourself more energised to action things you've avoided dealing with.

Cleaning up the physical part of your life can also help with clearing mental blockages or negative feelings. You can also add things into your physical space that you feel help keep the negativity out, such as candles, incense or other smells you like, or if you are more of a visual person you can use flowers or other things from nature that you connect with. You could create your own Midsummer broom on a large or small scale and hang it in your home to keep the good energy flowing.

26 • Bare feet
GROUNDING · ROOTS

Because Midsummer is often celebrated in the countryside with big fields of grass, country roads and soft surfaces, running barefoot is a common sight and something that is enjoyed by children as well as teens and adults.

Feeling nature's surface under your bare feet is about connecting with nature and Mother Earth. Feel your roots and where you come from, knowing that you are a part of the bigger whole. We are all connected to each other and to our planet, we all come from the same source and we all connect on the surface of the same planet. We all feel the warmth of the same sun and enjoy the light of the same moon and stars.

MESSAGE

This card is an indication that you may need to ground yourself and take a moment to stop and connect with your roots. Remember where you came from and what strengths you were born with and that you still have. You could re-connect with your support system, your family or your chosen family. They are all part of you.

Physically connecting with the land through your feet is a great way of grounding yourself. Feel the stability and the support you get from the earth. Envision yourself as a part of Mother Earth to access the strength she possesses.

27 • Celebration

HIGHLIGHT · EXCITEMENT

As with many other traditions Midsummer is rooted in Christianity and was originally a celebration of John the Baptist who was seen as a forerunner of Jesus Christ. However, in modern times it has become more of a large gathering to celebrate the summer solstice as it's seen as the beginning of the summer season with its bright nights and warm weather.

Regardless of the reasons behind celebrations and traditions, the common theme is the big gatherings and it's the people and the connections that make the day or event so special.

MESSAGE

You, too, can find things in your life worth celebrating. Think about who the people are that would make it extra special and would make you enjoy the cause even more.

Sometimes we are so set in our ways that we keep going on with life without noticing or celebrating our achievements. We celebrate the set dates that the calendar tells us to celebrate, yet there are rarely any new holidays or celebrations coming up in our calendars. That is not to say there aren't things worth celebrating.

We have forgotten a lot of the purposes and reasons behind many of the things we traditionally celebrate, and at the same time, we fail to celebrate new things that happen in our life that hold more personal value.

This card is an indication that you may have something in your life that deserves to be highlighted again, that should be brought to the surface and that people in your life need to enjoy with you. You deserve to enjoy the excitement of your achievements together with the ones you care about the most and that care about you.

28 · Sunset

CYCLE · ENDING

Even though the sun sets very late on Midsummer in the northern hemisphere we often experience it because of the late-night celebrations; sometimes we even get to experience both the sunset and the sunrise of the next day before the celebrations have finished and we've even slept.

MESSAGE

Sunset indicates the end of the day, the start of the night and the transition into a new day. Just like the sun cycles, so does your life. This card may be an indication that something positive has come to an end for you and you may not see the way out of it. But remember that you can see the ending of something as the beginning of something new. When the sun sets and then rises the next day, it may rise to become an even brighter day. Likewise, in your next chapter when the sun rises for you again, there may be something even better in store, you just had to go through the cycle in between.

The sun must go through the dark night to be able to rise again, so this card may reflect that you need to go through something difficult in order to come out on the positive side again. But this is all natural and a part of life and you can find comfort in knowing that whatever you are going through, it's part of a cycle and it will also come to an end.

29 ✦ Heat

ENERGY · VALUE

Midsummer usually marks the beginning of summer and for Scandinavian countries this means it's starting to get warm after a long winter. This is something highly appreciated by the vast majority and a reason to celebrate. We are not usually spoiled with heat and when the weather finally cracks and summer arrives it is something that everyone wants to make the most of.

You start seeing more and more people enjoying the outdoors: the parks and outdoor seating in restaurants are packed, people are out in their backyards and walking the streets enjoying the warmth. It is like this heatwave suddenly awakens the energy within and everyone starts to enjoy life a bit more.

MESSAGE

Wherever you are in the world and whatever weather or cycles you experience this is a message for you to find and appreciate the small things in life. Whether it's always around you or it's rare, make sure you see the value in it and feel it within.

It may not be about the weather for you; there can be other things in your life that don't come around very often or that come in a cycle and therefore are easy to miss, easy to forget or to see the value of. The more you can find appreciation and see the value of these things, the more you can enjoy your day-to-day life and make the most of it.

30 · Juicing
CHANGE · TRANSFORMATION

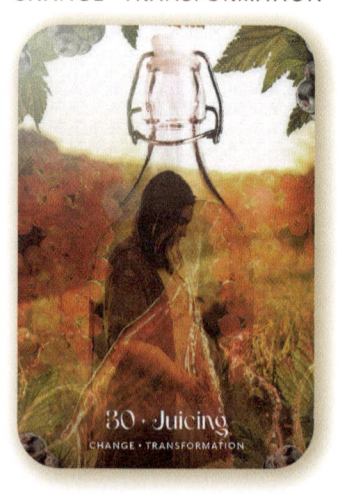

Since summer is a period of growth and bloom, there are many fruits and berries available for juicing. Elderflowers, blackcurrants, raspberries and strawberries are commonly made into juices around this time. The juicing process itself, where you transform the berries into liquid, can represent a deeper meaning. The earth is giving you something that you have the power to transform into something else. You get to be the alchemist in this process.

MESSAGE

This card may be an indication that you are going through changes in your life or that there are some changes that you need to make. You may have failed to see that you already have all the ingredients you need to create what you want and this is encouraging you to take a deeper look around to see what you have that might be of use to you.

Perhaps there are still some things you need to harvest in order to get the transformations happening. But remember that just as with juicing, you can be the alchemist of your life. You can take whatever you have and transform it into something else. You can use your skills, develop them and become something more. You can make changes to your home to transform your environment. Whatever it is you might need you can make it happen.

31 + Healing power
HEALING · TRANSITION

There are magical powers associated with Midsummer due to its close connection with nature and its celebration of the sun, warmth and growth during this period.

Midsummer brings positive energy while the blossoming of beautiful flowers, the running water in the streams and the heat of the sun bring healing power to the people.

The environment, the season and the holiday all provide the perfect conditions for rest, relaxation and healing.

MESSAGE

This card serves to remind you of the importance of taking a break and resting if you need to and having a relaxing moment for yourself to be able to heal, rejuvenate and gain new energy to move forward with.

The summer solstice represents the transition into a new and loved season and this indicates an opportunity for reflection and renewal.

Is there anything you need to clean out or release, whether it be energies, emotions or physical things to assist you in moving through this transitional period?

32 + Midsummer night's treasure
MYSTERY · PAST PRESENT FUTURE

Midsummer is associated with many rituals. Whether it be games, eating, singing or more traditional ceremonies, there is also space for you to make up your own traditions, rituals or games. One personal Midsummer ritual I used to engage in as a child was hiding special objects in nature, visible only if you knew about it but to other people it wouldn't be anything to take note of. It was a treasure of the night as it was placed when it was getting dark to invoke a sense of mystery.

This provided a sense of seclusion, of feeling special and being a part of something bigger with the group of people that were in the same pact of hiding. The objects then served as a reminder of this all the way through the year. It was like planting a seed of a feeling that lasted forever.

MESSAGE

Let this card be a reminder to you that even the smallest things can have a big impact and what you sow today you benefit from in the long run. See what you can do today that will serve as a reminder throughout the year of what you want to achieve, what you appreciate or just something to remind yourself that you are special.

Let it serve as a reminder to cherish the present moment as well as the past and the future.

33 • Future divination
CLARITY · GUIDANCE

Midsummer has a long history of being associated with divination and different techniques might be used, such as dream reading, the ritual of collecting flowers to place under your pillow to dream of who your future love would be or reading runes or tea leaves. It was believed that Midsummer had magical powers and therefore lent itself as the perfect timing for communicating with spirit or accessing the divine.

It was also believed that the powerful energy of the long-lasting daylight sun could enhance accuracy and clarity in divinations.

MESSAGE

You may never know for sure what will happen in the future or fully trust the readings you get, but you can still benefit from the energy of divination and gain insight into your own consciousness. With aid from whichever divination technique you prefer to use you can access your unconscious mind and bring things into light that may have been lurking in the darkness.

Let the powerful energy of the midnight sun guide you at this moment and use this card as a motivation to prepare for what's to come. Try and gain new insight or clarity to find a deeper understanding of yourself and plan accordingly.

34 · Dress

THE DIVINE · FEMININITY

In Sweden, the Midsummer celebration is steeped in tradition, with clothing playing an important role. National costumes representing each of the 28 states were traditionally worn, crafted from similar materials and featuring block colours of red, blue, yellow and green and often adorned with floral patterns. Women donned dresses while men wore pants and a shirt with a vest or jacket. Although some still wear these traditional costumes in formal settings, casual and modern clothing has become the norm for private celebrations.

Nowadays, a typical Midsummer dress is often flowy and lightweight, in a single colour or floral or nature-inspired patterns. The dress is not just a garment but a symbol of celebration, femininity, grace and elegance.

MESSAGE

This card encourages you to embrace your feminine energies, especially if you've been stuck in masculine energy for too long. Today, masculine energy tends to be task-focused and achievement-oriented. Nurturing, creativity and collaboration are some feminine energies to focus on regardless of your gender.

A dress can also be a symbol of spirituality and is often seen in religious or spiritual settings. It can represent a connection with the divine, goddesses and higher power. In modern times a dress is a common item worn daily and can provide a continuous reminder to connect with higher energies and the goddess within yourself. Hence, let the presence or use of a dress serve as a reminder to tap into your inner goddess and access the power within.

35 ✦ Spirits and drinks
REFRESHMENT · RITUAL

There is no celebration without an abundance of refreshments to choose from. Drinking is a ritual in itself with liquid running through your body, your body digesting it then taking up the energy of the contents.

MESSAGE

This card indicates that you might need some uplifting to renew or refresh something in your life. A drinking ritual can be of benefit and you can use it to bring focus to what actions you need to take.

Whatever spirit you choose, pay attention to the ingredients and what characteristics they possess. What is the meaning of them? How do they relate to your life currently? Imagine all the ingredients flowing through your body along with the liquid as you drink it and imagine how those qualities embody within you.

This card could also mean that there is something in your life that needs a revamp, a cleanse or even needs to be poured out completely. If nothing immediately comes to your mind upon hearing those words, you may need to ponder and search deeper to find out what it is. A ritual could help you.

36 ✦ Midnight sun
CREATIVITY · BONDING

The reason we celebrate Midsummer is the summer solstice, when the day is the longest and the night the shortest. This means that even at midnight it is still bright outside. In some locations very far north you can see the sun go down only for it to come right back up again. The midnight sun gives a special, magical feeling: as if you are invincible. The night is constantly young and there are so many possibilities of what can happen, where the night can go and what else you can plan for the night. It really opens your mind, searching for adventure and excitement.

MESSAGE

Channel the energy of the midnight sun and embrace your creative mind. What is it in your life that you want more of? Is there something new you would like to try? How can you bring more excitement into your life at this very moment without going too far out of what is already known to you?

This magical energy also provides the opportunity to bond even further with your friends. When you create something together under this magical energy field of the midnight sun there is an opportunity to grow stronger together. So who is your partner in crime? Is there anything you can do to deepen that connection you already have and grow even stronger together?

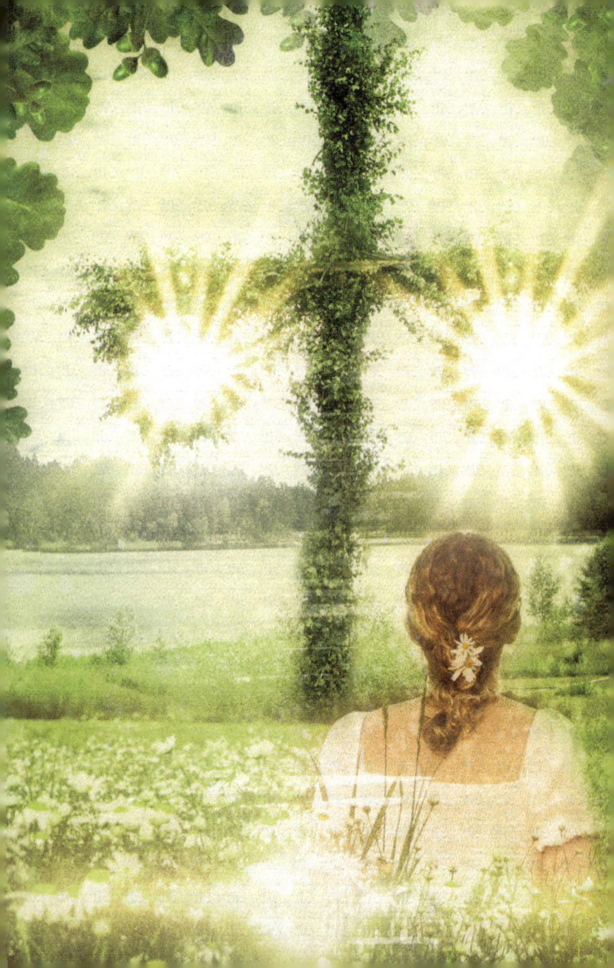

About the Creator

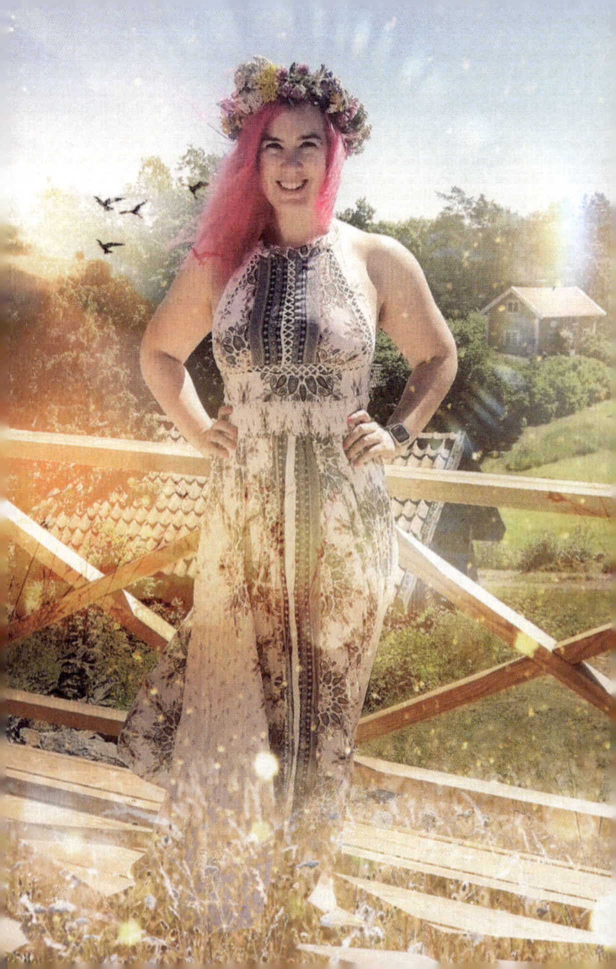

Hailing from Sweden and currently living in Sydney, Australia, Selena Moon has celebrated Midsummer for as long she can remember. It's a tradition close to her heart with many great memories and feelings that have inspired this deck.

Selena has been interested in art, drawing and technology since childhood and any free subject choices in school always tended towards the creative ones.

She has her own design studio and years of experience with freelance design work that evolved to include illustrations and digital art. Selena now has an established and successful career as a graphic designer, illustrator and digital artist in both Sweden and Australia.

Her art is a mixture of digital collage, drawings and line art to create unique, bold, colourful and highly detailed imagery. She finds inspiration from various avenues and likes to explore new fields so she doesn't get bound by the same style or technique, utilising her many skills in combination to create unique pieces.

With an interest and study in psychology she combines her knowledge, own experiences and tools with her passion for art to create products that inspire and motivate people in their lives. What motivates her most to create art is the notion that it can help people, that the creations will have a purpose and potential to affect other people in a positive way.

Find out more at selenamoon.co or on Instagram: @selena.moon.artist

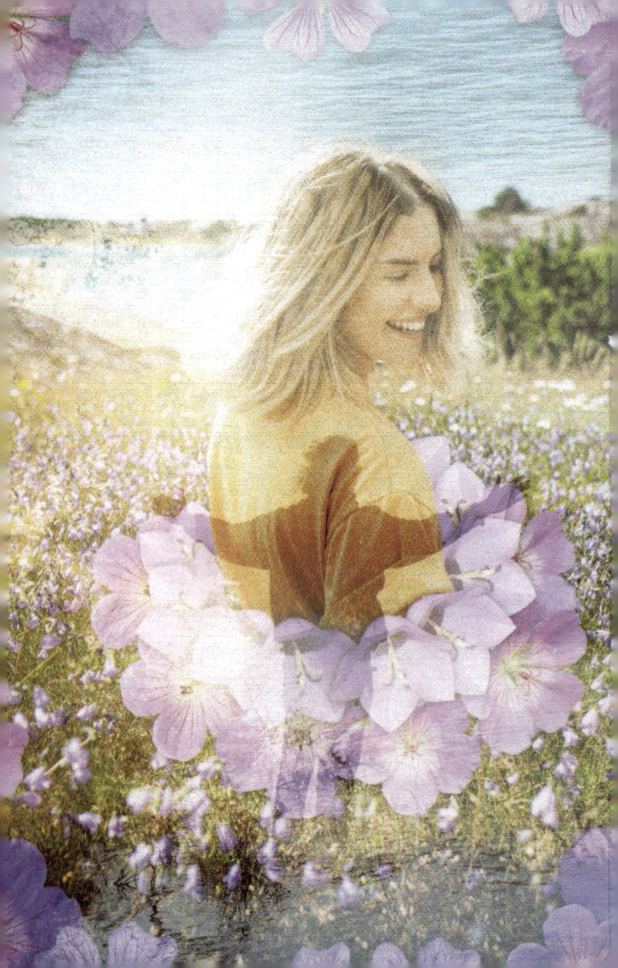